The
Monologues

Rebecca Russell
and Jenny Wafer

A SAMUEL FRENCH ACTING EDITION

SAMUEL FRENCH

FOUNDED 1830

SAMUELFRENCH.COM
SAMUELFRENCH-LONDON.CO.UK

ISBN 978-0-573-13019-9

www.SamuelFrench.com
www.SamuelFrench-London.co.uk

FOR PRODUCTION ENQUIRIES

UNITED STATES AND CANADA
Info@SamuelFrench.com
1-866-598-8449

UNITED KINGDOM AND EUROPE
Plays@SamuelFrench-London.co.uk
020-7255-4302/01

Each title is subject to availability from Samuel French, depending upon country of performance. Please be aware that THE REGINA MONOLOGUES may not be licensed by Samuel French in your territory. Professional and amateur producers should contact the nearest Samuel French office or licensing partner to verify availability.

MUSIC USE NOTE

Licensees are solely responsible for obtaining formal written permission from copyright owners to use copyrighted music in the performance of this play and are strongly cautioned to do so. If no such permission is obtained by the licensee, then the licensee must use only original music that the licensee owns and controls. Licensees are solely responsible and liable for all music clearances and shall indemnify the copyright owners of the play(s) and their licensing agent, Samuel French, against any costs, expenses, losses and liabilities arising from the use of music by licensees. Please contact the appropriate music licensing authority in your territory for the rights to any incidental music.

IMPORTANT BILLING AND CREDIT REQUIREMENTS

If you have obtained performance rights to this title, please refer to your licensing agreement for important billing and credit requirements.

THE REGINA MONOLOGUES was first presented by Tidemark Theatre at the Abbey Theatre, St. Albans on 10th July 2004. The performance was directed by Rosemary Goodman and the cast was as follows:

CATHY . . . . Rebecca Russell

ANNIE . . . . Anna MacLeod

JANE . . . . .Madison Hughes

ANNA . . . . Julie Grant

KATIE . . . . .Louisa Stevens

KATHERINE . . . . .Tina Swain

CHARACTERS

CATHY, the discarded wife.

ANNIE, the faded beauty, worn out with partying.

JANE, pale and vulnerable, with an air of simplistic naivety.

ANNA, looks older than her years. Striking and intelligent. Wears a wig.

KATIE, sometimes vulnerable and childlike, sometimes the assured teenager.

KATHERINE, the composed widow, determined and single-minded.

SUGGESTED CUTS

The authors are happy for certain cuts to be made to enable the piece to run under one hour. The suggested cuts are as follows:

p.10: (**CATHY**) "so I always used to glance over...see who's arriving."

"He said that he felt it too...But it was."

"I mean, I'd just taken...you can't refreeze those, can you?"

(**JANE**) "I'm so lucky. He's just so lovely."

p.11: (**ANNA**) "There!...buy London Rubber Company."

"And with the internet thing...get a transformation."

"Non-smoker who likes children and small animals."

p.13: (**CATHY**) "No one could fault...I can tell you."

p.15: (**JANE**) "But someone said...And very handsome."

p.18: (**ANNIE**) "I hope it's a boy...to shag them."

p.21: (**CATHY**) "Worse, I think I've really lost him now."

p.27: (**ANNIE**) "I was ever so slightly...When I staggered out"

p.28: (**JANE**) "Of course...He is my life."

p.30: (**CATHY**) "I could have had...Oh God, not him."

p.31: (**ANNIE**) "But I won't...(*Tries to laugh, but can't*)"

For our families

THE REGINA MONOLOGUES

(Scene: A room in which all the wives of one man have lived in their time. It is sparsely but richly set, in colours suggesting a faded opulence. There is a double bed centre stage, a screen upstage right draped with clothing, a chair next to the bed upstage right, a rocking chair upstage left, a dressing table and chair downstage left, a low coffee table at the front of the stage and floor cushions downstage right. All of these stations provide a start and finish for the monologues. A large, empty gilded frame hangs over the bed.)

(There is one of everything set – one wine glass, one handbag, one set of make-up, one pregnancy book, one magazine etc. The **QUEENS** *share and make use of the appropriate objects during their monologues. Their actions may be linked, e.g. one* **QUEEN** *pours a glass of wine from which another later drinks.* **CATHY** *also wears a ring which is passed from* **QUEEN** *to* **QUEEN** *at the end.)*

(The **QUEENS** *remain on stage most of the time, occasionally leaving for a quick costume change. They subtly carry on with their activities during the other monologues.)*

*(Effects music – '**REMEMBER ME MY DEAR**' by The Hilliard Ensemble fades into '**GREENSLEEVES**'. Lights soft but with focus on the empty frame)*

*(Effects music '**GREENSLEEVES**' fades into '**LOVE ME OR LEAVE ME**' by Nina Simone. Lights up. The wives enter one by one and end up at each of the stations. They are each oblivious to the presence of the others.)*

CATHY. Golden hair. That was the first impression I had. Golden, with just a touch of red. Like a halo. And a laugh so huge that it seemed to fill the air with a life of its own…the sort of person who leaves behind a hole in a room when he goes out.

He was only eighteen when I first met him. He'd just arrived from Luton. It was my late shift at the bar and the bus stop was just opposite, outside the Palace Hotel, so I always used to glance over, you know, see who's arriving. I was clearing tables as usual, wiping away spilt San Miguel and stale paella. Then I saw Him, getting off the bus. He was laughing, a god amongst the rest of the plebs. I couldn't take my eyes off him. I knew absolutely that here was my future, the ghost of my life to come. I had to have that man. He said that he felt it too, that instant attraction, which sounds really clichéd when you call it love at first sight. But it was. And it was all a bit tricky really as I was due to marry his brother the next day. We had to go through with it. I mean, I'd just taken all those breaded mushrooms out of the freezer, and you can't refreeze those, can you?

ANNIE. I've got this new phone. He gave it to me. Had it for a week now, still can't figure out how to phone my mum. Not that I'm not grateful. But I didn't really need a new phone, just a new number. What with the calls I'm getting from her. Really nasty. Abusive.

OK, so you can't blame her. I mean, I'm not entirely stupid, I can see it from her point of view. Married, not getting any younger, stuck by him through thick and thin, and then when she's just about past it herself, wham! He turns around and says he's leaving her. Only it wasn't really wham! It was months, years. And I really can't believe she didn't know.

JANE. I'm so lucky. He's just so lovely. Honestly, I'm so happy. He's just…you know…so lovely and thoughtful. And he makes me feel as if I'm the only woman he's ever loved. The only woman in the universe. I bet his first two wives never felt like this.

The thing is, he says…this is so sweet…that it's as if he mistook the first two for me, like when you're searching a crowd for the face you love. Even though he didn't know me then, didn't know I existed, it was me he was looking for. He saw them first and…and married them. But he always knew he'd find me one day. And now he has. And he's just…so lovely. I'm so happy. I'm so lucky.

ANNA. *(setting up a laptop)* There! Lock up your menfolk, sell pork belly and buy London Rubber Company.

It's really amazing isn't it, the potential in this little box. Recipes for anything from cherry scones to semtex. You can find anything, buy anything. My friend Gudrun found the man of her dreams on hers. Russian. Built like Adonis and with a touch as sensitive as a cotton top sheet. Can't speak a word of English, mind, but then who needs words when you have a dick the size of Gibraltar? And the good thing about this way of doing things is that you fall in love with the inner self before you see the real person. No preconceptions. And with the internet thing it'll be at least a few months before I have to meet him so that'll give me time to lose a couple of pounds, get a transformation.

Enter your personal details. That's the toughest bit. What you put in here makes all the difference. Oh, bollocks. Fun-loving…blonde. No! *(Beat)* Fun-loving, shapely blonde, mid…mmm…twenties seeks sensitive older man for friendship. Must share interests in… *(looks around for inspiration.)*…food. Food and fine wine and EastEnders. No! Theatre, classical music and keep fit. Non-smoker who likes children and small animals. Good sense of humour essential.

(Effects beep of mobile phone)

KATIE. *(receiving a text)* What?!

(Reads) Oh, no way! No way! Oh my God. Caz, you are such a slapper.

(Effects beep)

Shit. I mean he could have had anything.

(Types) "U cud b prgnt..."

(Effects beep)

Silly cow, I mean what is the point of wasting your life on some sixteen year old? Eh?

(Effects beep)

(Reads) "Have got morning after pill. Might as well save it till after tonight so can see what Jimmy's like as well..."

(Types) "...and what about STDs????"

For God's sake. See, my mom always said that I could do what I liked as long as I was sensible. She even gave me a pack of three the first time I went out on a date and my mates were like, amazed, because she was so cool and she said, 'well, I don't want to become a granny yet, Katie, so for God's sake take care'. And, like that's so right. She went with me to the docs as well so as I could go on the pill but even so, I always get the bloke to use a condom because the last thing I want right now is to die of AIDS or get chlamydia, become infertile and piss blood, you know?

(Effects beep)

(Reads) "Don't worry so much. Live a little."

Well, if she's not worried 'bout herself then why should I worry? I'd better get ready to go over to Sharma's, she's got a load of new tops and she says I can borrow one to go with my new skirt for Tommo's party tonight and we're going to do fake tan first, so I've got to find my razor as well before I go. Shit, where did I put it?

KATHERINE. People have often asked me why I seem to prefer older men. Of course, I never tell them the truth. I always say, 'Oh my dear, age has nothing to do with love'. And I suppose in a way that's true. But it has everything to do with lust. Or the absence of it. Three marriages, widowed twice. Once an accident, twice a tragedy...and three times? Some would say jolly good luck.

Provided that the assets are healthy enough, the main consideration, when trying to decide whether or not to marry a man significantly older than oneself, is whether one would be prepared, if absolutely necessary, to wipe his arse for him. You know, assuming the worst. And I have to admit that it was rather touch and go in the arse department this time. Frankly, I thought that his suppurating leg wounds were more than enough for any woman. However, on reflection, I felt that his bank balance more than compensated for his anus horribilis. *(She laughs at her little joke.)* And here we are!

You see, being very rich and about to die makes any man practically irresistible to women.

(Effects music **'QUEEN FOR TONIGHT'** *by Helen Shapiro. Lights to 50%.* **QUEENS** *move to different station. Lights up.)*

CATHY. It was a lovely wedding. Everyone said so, even if I'm sure they said differently behind my back. They were even running a sweepstake at the back of the hall, you know, over how long it would last.

No one could fault the day though. Perfect weather, the church filled with Calla lilies, and me, looking radiant. Well bloody right I did! I had most of the Elizabeth Arden counter slapped on my face. I wasn't taking any chances with open pores, I can tell you.

Oh, I knew what they were all thinking. Snide digs about the older bride...nobody bats an eyelid if a man marries a woman younger than himself, but a woman marries a younger man and they're straight on the phone to Esther bloody Rantzen.

But he didn't care. He watched me walking up that aisle as if I were the only woman in the universe. All that pilates and botox had finally paid off and it was definitely worth it, just to see the look in his eyes.

He made a lovely speech at the reception. Really moving, about how he missed his older brother on this special day, but knew that, if he'd been able to make it, he would have raised his glass and blessed us both. I even had a bit of a weep. Silly, really, as had his older brother been there, and not six foot under, then I wouldn't have been getting married at all, because I would still have been married to him. The brother. So there would been no special day on which to miss him…

Of course, it was tragic. We'd only been man and wife for a few months. But, you know, he was never what you might call the picture of health. Rather small, really, and pale, with skinny legs and a bit of a pigeon chest thingy going on. Not a bit like his brother, who sat there at the reception like Adonis. And I thought, well, if his brother's looking down on us now, I'm sure he'd be comforted to see me in such good hands. Keeping it in the family, so to speak. Yes! He'd have liked that, I'm sure.

ANNIE. You'd have to be stupid, wouldn't you? Not to know. Most women I know could spot an affair before it even started. They start brushing their teeth before they go out, fresh underwear without so much as a prompt – and the toenails! Christ! The minute they stop lacerating your calves in bed with their grotty, neglected keratin, you practically have absolute proof. Then there are the receipts. Only your skilled adulterer discards telltale receipts. Your average, first-time adulterer keeps them. Doesn't give them so much as a passing thought. And you'd find them, wouldn't you? Next time you put his jeans in the wash. In there, amongst the fluff and the multiplying microbes and the Twix wrappers. Evidence of illicit lunches caught forever in carbon paper, just waiting to be found. Asking for it.

JANE. I've had the scan, and...it's a boy! But someone said a really mean thing to me. She said, thank goodness it's a boy, because if the baby has to look like its dad, then being a boy will be a blessing. Well, she didn't actually say it to me, she said it to my stepdaughter, who, to give her credit, stood up for her dad. It's not true anyway. Oh, I know he's put on weight now, but I've seen pictures of when he was young. Golden hair. Honestly, golden. And very handsome.

When I told him I was pregnant...this is so sweet. He went straight out and bought a little, tiny football shirt. And I said, what if it's a girl? And he said that I had given him everything he dreamed of and he didn't see why I would stop now.

I'm not going to tell him that I know for definite. I'm going to keep it secret. I'm so lucky.

ANNA. Bloody hell! Fifty-four responses in twenty-four hours. There are some right saddos out there, aren't there? Present company excepted, *naturellement*. I've cut out all the ones who still live with their parents, all those who list being a friend of a tank museum high amongst their hobbies and all those who generally look like axe murderers from their photos and now I'm left with three. Not a bad day's work, though. Number one says that he is looking for a special someone to travel the world with and who can take an interest in the smaller things in life with him. Mmmmm, possibly has very small dick. Number two would also like to meet a special someone to venture into the sunset years with. Likes chess and good conversation. Physical relationship secondary to spiritual bonding. Uh huh, can't get it up. Now, number three looks a bit more like it. Passionate, musical and artistic male seeks partner to share life, fortune and bed. Looks a bit ginger in the photo but it's probably just the flash. Beggars can't be too choosy, can I? Well hello, number three, you lucky, lucky man!

KATIE. He was ever so nice. Really friendly, and not a bit, you know, up himself. I thought he might be, the way Mum went on about how rich he is and how well he's done for himself and how if I played my cards right he might be able to help all of us.

Did I say he's got a pool? Fantastic. We all went in, even Dad. Poor old Dad. He was a bit uptight on the way there...I think it was the car. Not our car, the one sent to pick us up! Yeah, leather seats, silver Mercedes convertible – amazing. I just loved being in that car. And when we got to the house, there were these electronic gates and this fantastic sound of crunching gravel. And the house, all white, pillars everywhere. Imagine me being related to that lot, and no one telling me till I'm almost sixteen!

'Course, he's not really my uncle. He said not to call him Uncle, just to use his first name, 'cos he's only a distant relative. So I did. Dad didn't like it; he's really tight about what he calls "over familiarity."

It did feel weird at first. I mean, he's quite old...and fat. I've seen photos of him when he was young; they're all over his house. He was well fit. But now he's...well... fat. And he sweats really badly...and he's ginger. I'm just glad he didn't get into his trunks. He just watched us all from his lounger. He had on this cream linen suit. He said I could come over any time, just to let him know and he'll send a car. He said he'd let me use the sauna.

How cool is that?

KATHERINE. It's the children I feel sorry for. All that chopping and changing. Troops of women trying to find different euphemisms for stepmother. Or not even pretending that they care, like that nasty little piece he had for a second wife. But I'm not one to gossip.

I try to remain...even. No gushing, but I'm there if they need me. A sympathetic, objective ear. I think it helps – the fact that I have no children of my own.

Taking on other women's children is rather like taking on a failing school; you've got to drag the little sods up by their ears.

The girls are...difficult. The younger one is clever, of course, and she'll need to be, with that hair and a forehead you could land a helicopter on. The other one is as wilful as they come. And the boy? Poor little chap. Not very strong. Asthmatic.

They'll soon learn that things are better, with me around.

(Effects music 'BABY BABY ALL THE TIME' – Diana Krall. Lights to 50%. QUEENS *move to a different station. Lights up.)*

CATHY. *(upside down with legs raised on the bed, counting)* Fifty-seven monkeys, fifty-eight monkeys, fifty-nine monkeys, sixty monkeys. *(Laughs)* God, if that won't do it, nothing will. Fifteen minutes post-coitus upside down and a banana. *(Grabs banana and peels, starts to eat)* See, if you want a boy you have to eat food shaped like a willy. Bananas, sausages, courgettes...marrows! Bloody hell! No, I'm only joking now! And of course, the upside down bit just encourages those sperm without a sense of direction, which, let's face it, is most of the little shits, to swim upstream, as it were. Egg-bound, so to speak. Until gravity does its bit and then you're stuffed. Or, more to the point, not stuffed. Oh bugger. No, I can't get upset, that would be counter-effective, mess my hormonal balance up. And I've already had one child, so, you know, it can't be that bad; I mean – everything functioned once upon a time. And I've still got my health, so it's only a matter of time, really. And today is day eleven, so we've still got days thirteen and fifteen. Even for a girl, odd for a boy. It's got to work this time. Because I've not had any alcohol, I don't smoke, and I've tried hard not to think bad thoughts. Although I may have lapsed once. Or twice. Oh, God, don't get upset, breathe, breathe, relax, relax, relax. There. You see? Think calm thoughts, walking along a path by a rippling brook. The stream breaking gently over the pebbles, worn smooth with time. A thrush sings in the trees above me. In the distance a church bell sounds. That's better. Oh, I know for a fact that he's fathered at least one little brat without so much as a single wedding vow, and if those tarts can manage it, why the hell can't I? Eh, God? Are you listening? I do everything right, keep the commandments; arrange the altar flowers, pray! And yet where the hell are you when I need you? I'll even be happy if it's ginger. Please?

ANNIE. I'm pregnant. That didn't take long, did it? I reckon the sperm were so bloody relieved not to have to put up with his first wife's wizened ovaries that they just went right ahead and had a party. Bet they were fighting over the privilege of fertilizing my lovely, ripe eggs.

Sorry. Do I sound smug? Gloating? Triumphant? Good. I'm making the right impression, then.

At the wedding, you could tell that none of his lot gave it more than a year. This'll wipe the smirks off their faces. Especially if it's a boy. Heir to the family business, carrying on the family name and all that. I hope it's a boy. You know where you are with boys, like dogs. Feed them, exercise them, and then, when they're old enough, find some silly bitch to shag them.

Actually, I don't care what it is. As long as it's healthy. No, that's not true. Come on, Annie, be honest, you want a boy to get one over on her. The First Wife.

He's a good dad to his little girl, though, despite the divorce. I really think that this baby will bring us closer. Not that we're having problems; like I say, the sex is great. But a child…well, it'll make everything more permanent. Oh, I know he won't leave me, don't worry about that. I've got enough tricks up my nightie to keep him entertained for years. And when we have a son, we'll be a unit. Like he was with her. His first wife.

JANE. Only three months to go. I've stopped being sick now. Apparently with most women it stops by week fourteen. So I was only sick for an extra ten weeks. And he's been so sweet about it. I mean, I haven't been able to eat meat, or anything really, just the smell of meat made me ill, and he loves meat. So, what he did was, he's had lots of pool parties, so he could barbeque. In the fresh air. And he suggested I sleep at the back of the house, so the smell didn't float up.

The pool is quite new. He has a lot of people over. He knows a lot of people. I don't mind. He's naturally gregarious, whereas I … I'm happy with just him.

I haven't been in the pool yet. I'd feel like a whale in fancy dress. But he says…this is really sweet…that I look beautiful to him, because I'm carrying his son.

Oh, I told him, in the end. He was going to have the nursery painted blue anyway, so I thought that the element of surprise…well, there didn't seem much point. And I'm glad I told him, because he was so happy.

He's spent a fortune. The cot was imported from somewhere I can't pronounce, in Germany or somewhere, and it has a special thing built in which detects any change in baby's body heat or breathing pattern. And he's had a mural painted of him and his…his son, in the park, riding bikes, playing football, taking over a multi-national company…actually, I made that one up.

I'm in the mural, too. There's a house on a hill, all white, with a swimming pool, and if you look at the top left hand corner, in the window, I'm there.

I'm waving.

I've chosen the music for the birth. I'm having Ravel's *Bolero*, and baby is having sounds of the womb piped through, you know, for continuity. The birth will be a moment of tranquillity for mother and child.

I'm not going to have pain relief. I want to be there, in the moment, for the birth of his son. It's going to be so exciting. I can't wait.

ANNA. Well, I think I got away with it. I deliberately chose Bar Med on account of the low voltage halogen lighting. Very flattering. Especially that electric blue tinge and I sat at the end of the bar, back to the mirror on a bar stool which showed my legs off a treat. Let's just say he noticed that too. Couldn't take his eyes off them and when he did they only made it as far north as my cleavage, which I have to admit is rather a *pièce de resistance*. He wasn't quite what I expected though. Quite chunky in a muscly sort of way. And very strong jawline, which generally shows a sensitive side, so that's nice. The only slight downside as far as I could see was that he is actually ginger. Normally, I wouldn't go for that type but, quite frankly, his other assets outweigh the ginger thingy. He would appear to be very, very rich.

KATIE. *(upset and scared)* I'm never going back there again, never. Oh my God, he makes my skin crawl. I've had four showers and I can still feel his fat, sweaty hands on me. And he said I shouldn't tell anyone, says it would be really bad if I did. Oh God, what can I do? I was in the pool, just like before but my dad left me this time, said Uncle would run me home after my swim. It had been so hot at school so it was really nice to cool off. But when I got out, I went to get showered and I didn't see him, but he followed me into the bathroom and he was naked behind me and he's so big that I couldn't get past him to get my towel, and I just wanted my towel. He said that I should let him help to wash off the chlorine because it would dry my skin out and that I should close my eyes and just enjoy it. He started to lather me and I screamed and he put his soapy hand over my mouth and told me not to scream because it would be bad if I did. And he started to touch me and it was horrible and his fat stomach was pimply and covered in freckles, and oh my God, his, his...thing was huge and it kept touching me. And he wants me to go back there after school next week. And I'm so scared because if I don't he says he won't help Dad with the business and we really need his help. And I think I'd rather be dead.

KATHERINE. Those fucking children! I swear that if they don't go, I will, and bugger the inheritance.

The girls are the worst. Sniggering, telling lies about me, texting each other all the time, even at meals. I try to feel sorry for them, really. I know it can't be easy, being the one whose mother was dumped for a slut with the morals of an alley cat, or being the daughter of the slut. And that boy... I know he lost his mother in tragic circumstances, but does he have to be so wet? Drooping around the house, coughing all the time... at least he's not getting any stronger. No chance of him causing much trouble.

I'll definitely have to watch the girls, though. They ask their father too many questions. Left to himself, he's very easy. Malleable, almost. Quite happy to sign anything so long as I keep the house filled with young women. Oh, he only looks these days. Lies transfixed by the pool. Just looking. Touching would bring on a coronary.

Of course, it helps that he is actually richer that even I realised.

(Effects music: 'YOU'VE CHANGED' by Ella Fitzgerald. Lights to 50%. QUEENS *move to different station. Lights up.)*

CATHY. Things aren't going very well. I don't think he finds me attractive any more. Worse, I think I've really lost him now. I thought that he'd buy in to IVF big time, because the doctor's up for being bunged a few extra quid to put back only male embryos. But apparently the idea of his own, instant five-a-side squad doesn't seem to do it for him any more. It comes to something when the bastard can't even be arsed to wank into a pot for me. Christ! Do you know how humiliating that is? He's in a room with a pile of girlie mags and he can't even do that one small thing for me. OK, I know it's not nice, having a queue of people outside watching you go into 'the' room, everyone of them knowing what you're going to be doing for the next three minutes to God knows how long. And I am sympathetic to a point, but come on, compared with having huge, willy-shaped cameras shoved in to take pictures of your ovaries, or daily injections which make you feel like shit and then being raided by a needle the size of an umbrella to get the eggs out. And then, shoving them back in and drugs to keep your womb going and if you're lucky, nine months of sickness, swollen everythings, high blood pressure, piles, peeing every fifteen seconds and finally – labour! Well compared to that, a wank is a walk in the park. And on top of that, he thinks I'm stupid. Thinks I don't know about her. Little wonder he can't perform for me if he's shagging that slapper every second he can. Well, I've got news for them. They're not that clever, I've known for months. Ever since I found a receipt for a cosy little lunch for two at the Queens' Head.

ANNIE. I've been in the bath for three hours. Me and twenty chamomile tea bags. It's supposed to help with the stitches. Now I smell like cat's pee, but I still can't sit down without putting a cushion in the fridge first.

When it was all over, I asked if I needed any stitches. Being ignorant of medical sub-text, I took their silence to mean no. What it actually meant was they were sending out for reinforced nylon thread and a Black and Decker. Two hours, it took them. They had time to do a 'home sweet home' cross-stitch down there. My perineum virtually had to be reconstructed from scratch. I half expected them to ask if I had a photo of what it used to look like. I don't, but I know a man who does, I'd have said.

Was he there? Was he fuck. Off out as soon as I stopped dilating and started screaming. I'd already made my mind up that I'd scream. If you don't then they might think it's easy, and then where would you be for emotional blackmail?

We haven't got a name for it yet. It's healthy, all right, but no willy. I tried to feed her, but... I don't know, I just couldn't get on with it. And she has this way of looking at me, out of these pale eyes, as if she knows. She knows she's not what I wanted, but doesn't care.

It's not my fault. It's the man decides the sex of the baby, all I've got is a heap of X chromosomes just waiting for a Y to come along. And it's definitely not my fault that she's ginger. That's definitely him.

(Effects lights to cold blue spot with 6ft spill over the bed)

JANE. *(on the bed, panting heavily in the final stages of childbirth.)* Aaaaah! Christ! *(In between contractions)* If I come back again, I'm bloody coming back as a wombat or some other sodding marsupial. Because then the baby can crawl out of my womb at a few weeks' old, latch on the outside and carry on growing in a roll of fat somewhere rather than me having to push it out through a 10-centimetre hole when it's the size of a small horse. *(Contraction starts to build up again)* Aaaargh! Christ! OK I'll have drugs now. Nurse!! Nurse! Get me drugs now. Aaargh! What do you mean too far gone? Don't you come all that bloody midwife crap with me, give me drugs. NOW!

(Effects lights back up)

ANNA. Well, I have to say I've had better reactions. And worse too. Christ, yes, I've definitely had worse reactions. A black eye, bloodied nose, cracked rib. There was a period where I thought they'd give me my own chair in A and E, I was in there that often.

You see, it's quite a tricky subject to broach. Puts 'Have you got a condom?' on a par with 'More tea, Vicar?'

It was all going swimmingly as well. We'd met in Bar Med again, same stool, same legs. I made sure he had a few more than me so that his perception would be ever so slightly challenged. Well, I needed a bit of a head start and it's every girl for herself I always say. Then supper at Casa Mia, a couple of pre-prandials, a *bouteille* or two and then I suggested dessert in bed. Now by this time he'd had enough to practically floor a hippo so I thought I'd be fairly safe. But I hadn't accounted for a liver the size of Torquay and the constitution of...well, a hippo, and consequently, he wasn't quite as sozzled as I thought. So without dragging out the sordid details any more, we dived into bed, ripped each other's clothes off, he groped all the necessary bits, shouted, 'She's snot amaidens!' and passed out on me shag pile.

KATIE. Mum took me shopping today. All the really posh, designer outlets, not the usual tat. I felt like Julia Roberts in *Pretty Woman*.

He told her to. Said, 'Take Katie shopping and get her fixed up with a decent wardrobe.' I don't like him calling me Katie. Only my best mates and my Mum call me Katie. I don't like him buying me stuff, either, but... Mum said it's only clothes. I almost told her there and then, but then... I don't want to make him angry.

Frankie wasn't that impressed, either. Frankie – that's my boyfriend. I almost told him last night. About the shower thing. Everything, you know? But I don't want to lose him. He's really special. Caz says I'm going soft, but she doesn't know how much it helps. I mean, I've never told anyone, about that time in the shower. He's tried it on a bit since then, nothing so bad though, and I mean it's not like he's ever going to try and...you know. That would be so gross. I sort of think, he's just a bit of a saddo.

Mum and Dad are out tonight, gone to have dinner by his bloody pool. He said he had a proposition. I hope he offers them money. Things with the business are really bad; we might have to sell the house. So I can't make trouble. Can I?

KATHERINE. If we knew what old age would bring on, we'd all book in for a spot of euthanasia at – say – fifty-ish. A dickey ticker is only the tip of the iceberg, believe me. Liver failure, kidney failure, obesity, diabetes, arthritis – in both knees – poor circulation and leg ulcers. To be honest, with a spouse like that, impotence is not only a blessing but the least of his worries. He went to the doctor because consummation was a bit of a problem. I told him that I didn't mind, that being near him was enough. More than enough. But eventually the doctor prescribed some little sticks. Muse, they're rather quaintly called. He was hoping for Viagra, just a simple pill to swallow, but apparently they didn't go with the heart problem. Well, he thought all his troubles were over and I thought mine were just beginning, when, as luck would have it, he read the little leaflet that comes in the box. Now, the instructions basically were that he had to shove this little stick into the end of his willy and squeeze the medication out, rolling 'it' between the palms of his hands to distribute the medication evenly, wait for the burning sensation to subside, carrying on rolling, and then after five to ten minutes he would, erm, have the capability to, well, you know, for thirty minutes. He practically ran screaming to the abbey to join the brotherhood there and then. My main concern, apart from the obvious, was what would we do for the other twenty-seven minutes? Boil nine eggs?

(Effects music: 'OTHER WOMAN' by Nina Simone. Lights to 50%. QUEENS move to different stations. Lights up.)

CATHY. The thought that I had the upper hand kept me going. I had the family home and the holiday home, the daughter, the trips abroad – the normal bit, you know? Because affairs aren't real. Not real life. They're as much a part of the imagination as they are day-to-day reality. They're a bit of escapism. A bit of fun. Enjoying sex again. Enjoying the mystery of another person, when you know your spouse so well that you hardly bother to talk any more. Don't need to. You drift apart, do your own separate things, but can't quite tear yourself away properly. And then this other person, the interloper, comes along and provides a bit of a distraction, fulfils that need for mystery, excitement, discovery, but doesn't ever present a proper threat because it's not real enough, not important enough to ever replace the spouse and all that history. Well, I got that wrong, didn't I? But if he thinks I'm going quietly, he's got another think coming. Why the bloody hell should I step down after all that loyal service? And how the hell could I? I can't start again. Not now. I can't face dating again and single bars and putting up with irrelevant chit-chat from losers who think you're bound to go for them, because you're older and single and therefore desperate. I can't go back to small talk, and fumbling with a stranger's body in the dark, and believe me, it would have to be the dark with my thighs. I can't do it. I just can't. *(Beat)* Because I love him.

ANNIE. He's sleeping. Rolled off me five minutes ago and he's sleeping like a baby. A baby warthog, that is, with acute adenoidal distress, but still – it's good to know he's at peace.

I know I sound bitter; I should be grateful I suppose. Full of wifely gratitude that he's managed to get it up at all. I mean, let's face it, it's becoming a bit of a problem. My problem, of course, for not being sexy enough to ignite the fire in his middle-aged loins.

The joke is, I still fancy him. The man I seduced, who seduced me. Trouble is, there's no shortage of women younger then me who are quite prepared to flash their thongs at a man, beer belly and all, if he's as rich as my husband is.

I hope that's all it is. I hope it's just money. I can cope with gold-diggers, women who just want the thrill of being wined, dined and screwed by the man who owns the hotel. That kind of greed is fine by me. There are plenty of Late Room bookings to go round.

What I'm afraid of is another woman like me. One who'll hold out for more.

It might have been different if only I hadn't miscarried. It was a boy, of course, fair-haired, fair skinned. I just felt so empty. My dreams for the future, my insurance, just sliding out of me like that.

There's this girl. I saw him talking to her at the company dinner dance. I was ever so slightly bladdered, well; it's the only thing that gets me through. And I had to go to the loo to throw up – I was just pregnant, but didn't know it. I looked in the mirror and saw this raddled old hag, face red and shiny, tits stretch-marked like the skin on hot milk, hair like a tractor had driven over it. And then I realised it was me.

When I staggered out he was leaning over her, all protective and suave – well, a dinner jacket hides a multitude of sins. And she was just gazing up at him. Like I used to.

Oh God, what I'm really afraid of is another woman like me. A woman who'll fall in love with the bastard.

JANE. I did it. Didn't I? Yes, I did it. Where is he? Where is my son? What have you done with him? Why don't you bring him to me, let me see him?

No...it's all right. I remember. I've been ill, haven't I? I'm glad he wasn't... I'm glad he didn't come. I wouldn't have liked him to see me. And they said... *(She begins to cry.)* Where is he? Why doesn't he come? Does he know it's a boy?

Of course. He came. He kissed me. I remember. He cried. He held our son and he cried. *(She becomes more feverish, more delirious.)*

Where is he? Is my baby sick? Where's my husband, why doesn't he come? He must come, I love him. He is my life.

ANNA. Family folklore has it that I was an unusually quiet baby. Unnaturally quiet. Watchful, not crying when my feed was late, or my nappy needed changing. My mother couldn't decide whether I was a genius, or just odd.

It's still up for debate.

My grandmother, of course, was the one who found it most worrying. She said that crying was a sign of health, and that there must be something wrong with me.

Again, the jury's still out.

Everything hinged on my christening. Oh, yes, I was christened in the family robe. I've got a picture of me on a cushion, looking adorable. Always took a good picture, me. Three months old, but I've tilted my head towards the camera to hide any hint of a double chin.

Apparently, yelling your head off at a christening is a sign of crying the devil out, of getting rid of all those original sins.

But I remained silent throughout. My grandmother tutted, no doubt, and shook her head at this doom-laden omen. But they christened me anyway, in the name of the Father, the Son and the Holy Spirit.

(Removing her wig as she intones the names) Robert Charles Anthony. Good, solid names. But not, as it turned out, what I would have chosen.

KATIE. I've had a facial. And my nails done. And there's a hairdresser coming and a make-up artist. I feel like bloody J-Lo.

(Effects text bleep)

(Reads) "How r u?"

Caz.

(Types) "O.K."

I haven't seen Dad all morning. Isn't he supposed to be here, going all soppy at the thought of his little girl getting married?

(Effects text bleep)

(Reads) "R U Scared?"

Mum's like a cat on hot bricks. But she's loving it. Got a hat the size of a small planet.

(Types) Scared shitless.

The honeymoon's going to be in the Maldives. I didn't have a clue where it was, had to look it up at school, in the geography room. Course, I'm not going back into Year 12. I don't care. I've outgrown that lot.

(Effects text bleep)

Frankie. Oh, shit.

(Reads) "Hi how r u?"

(Types) "Told u not to call."

(Effects text bleep)

(Reads) "U dnt hv to do this"

Christ. What the fuck does he know?

(Types) "Leave me alone."

(Effects text bleep)

(Reads) "He's an old man u can't do this. I luv U"

I've got to do it. Everybody's waiting.

(Types) "Leave me alone."

Dad's in deep shit. He's been taking money from the company. I mean, he was desperate. 'Uncle' says that if I don't go through with it he'll go to the police and Dad could end up in prison. He says he knows people in there who'll do stuff to Dad. I can't let that happen.

(Effects text bleep)

I'm getting married.

KATHERINE. *(clearing clutter)* There's a glaring business opportunity for a far-sighted businessman or woman to provide a sensitive skip hire service for families hit by death. It just smacks of insensitivity to have a huge tatty yellow and blue bucket sat on one's drive waiting to be filled with unwanted possessions, doesn't it? What I'd like is a solemnly coloured, lined skip – no, 'receptacle' – with maybe a holder for a small, floral tribute to show due respect. I remember my grandmother saying that my mother, her daughter, would be hiring a skip the minute she breathed her last, to clear out her years of treasures. And she was right. Clutter, my mother called it, and she did just that, albeit after a slightly more respectable two days had passed. I thought she was callous at the time, but having lived through the death of two dear husbands so far, I can see the merit in a swift clear out. The things we keep. Knick-knacks, trifles, letters – my God! Why? Look, a letter here from one dead person to another. What is the point? Life goes on. Life goes on.

(Effects music 'PLAIN GOLD RING' by Nina Simone. Lights to 50%. QUEENS *move to different stations. Lights up.)*

CATHY. *(pouring wine)* You won't believe this, but I really think that if he had told me earlier it would have been much better. I mean in the long run. Much better in the long run. Oh, don't get me wrong, it would still have been humiliating and devastating…but I could have survived it. You see, I might have moved on back then, found someone else. I could have had more babies, I'm sure, if I'd found…

Because some people can manage that, you know. No arsing about with other people, actually keeping themselves unto themselves. But not him. Oh God, not him.

And now what? I'm stuck here in the back of bloody beyond, two trains and five sweaty tube stops to Harvey Nicks, whilst he—

But you know what, he says he stayed with me to 'preserve the family'. Hah! And I'm supposed to be grateful? Oh, I'm grateful all right! My ovaries have packed in, my laughter lines have become hysterical and my middle age spread is threatening to envelop Warwickshire. Who's going to look at me now? Oh, but thank God, the family was preserved!

ANNIE. He doesn't want me any more. Not to talk to, not to sleep with. Have I changed that much? He looked at me tonight and his eyes were cold. It was the way he used to look at her when I was first with him. Oh God. I think he... I think he's got someone else.

I'm scared. I'm... I don't get scared, not me, but that look... I almost felt pity for her when she was at the receiving end of it. What goes around...

But I won't go quietly, not like her. No cottage in Ludlow for me. I'll go down fighting. *(In a cockney accent)* As long as I go down, darlin'. *(Tries to laugh, but can't)* Nobody tells me to go; nobody pays me off with a little yearly allowance. He'll try to fix it; he'll get me done for adultery. He knows people who'll say anything he tells them...and then it's off to some fucking one-bedroomed flat for me, out of sight, out of mind, just like his first wife.

I may as well be dead.

JANE. *(writing a letter)* "I don't want you to mind, if Daddy finds someone else. I'd like him to, really. He's a wonderful, loving man, and someone like him should have someone to share life with. Of course, I wish that could be me, but if not, then I would like it to be a lovely, kind lady who will be a mummy to you too. I'm going to leave this letter with Daddy to give to you when you're eighteen. You'll understand everything then, I'm sure. I think my main advice to you would be to be loyal and fair and honest like your daddy. Do as you would be done by and you'll never go wrong. I'll always be with you, my sweet boy."

ANNA. Divorce? Can't recommend it highly enough. Get yourself a good settlement, keep things amicable and bingo! Set up for life as an independent woman. And, if he tries to cause trouble…well, he knows the tabloids would have a field day.

I sometimes wonder if it's because of me he went after that poor little cow. Had to prove he could still pull the real thing. She's so young – I don't see how even his bank balance could be enough to cushion the blow of waking up to that every morning, not at her age.

Anyway, not my problem. Me? I'd say I got off lightly.

I've got enough alimony to keep me in Chardonnay and Wonderbras for a lifetime. Worth it to sleep with that arrogant prick. *(Laughs)* And enough to say ta ta to mine next week.

KATIE. *(distraught)* This is really fucking with my head. I thought I could cope with him, touching me, you know, and when he couldn't do it on our wedding night, I was really, really glad. I tried to get out of it anyway, pretending to be asleep, saying I had my period you know? But nobody has that many periods, do they? And none of the other excuses sounded reasonable any more so I knew I'd eventually have to do it.

God, he's so fat and his skin is slimy all the time because he sweats so much. His shirt was practically wringing wet with the effort of climbing the stairs and when he climbed on top of me I just couldn't breathe. His breath stank when he kissed me, and when he tried to force his tongue in my mouth I could feel his nose hair. I just wanted to scream, 'Get the fuck off me!' My neck was hurting because I was crushed against the headboard with all the pushing and shoving. And it wasn't like with Frankie because I just wasn't ready and the more I thought about it the less I wanted it and he just got angry and kept me pinned down. I tried to close my legs and he just carried on. I started to cry and he just got angrier and that seemed to help him and it just hurt me more. And now, it really hurts when I go to the toilet and walk and I've been bleeding as well, and I'm so frightened that he'll want to do it again tonight. Oh God, I wish I was dead.

KATHERINE. I'd like to say he looked peaceful, but he didn't. More...sulky, like a child who was being made to do something he didn't want to.

It wasn't a peaceful death. I've seen many, and the worst are when the person involved fights the inevitable. He smelt dreadful, too. Body odour doesn't really add to that sense of awe which is so desirable at a deathbed.

But it's over. I've almost finished sorting out his personal effects. It's taken me a while. I found a letter, to his son from his mother. To be opened on his eighteenth birthday. Very badly written. I've disposed of it. No boy needs to know that his poor, dead mother was a sentimental airhead.

My friend Anthea's coming round tonight. We've been promising ourselves a little cruise for ages, and my recent bereavement has swelled the coffers admirably. Of course, the girls are screaming manipulation, but it'll never stand up in court. And it will do them good to have to learn to make their own way in the world. No woman should rely on a man to keep her.

A nice, long cruise. Just what I need. Of course, cruises do tend to attract the older, single man. Oh yes. I'm always, always open to the possibility of companionship – with the right man.

(Effects music: 'YOU CAN HAVE HIM' by Ella Fitzgerald.)

(CATHY takes a glass of wine back to the coffee table. Drops her diamond ring into it. Exit.)

(ANNIE is swallowing pills with vodka. Goes to wine glass, finishes wine and takes ring to JANE. Exit.)

(JANE is lying on the cushions. Takes ring to ANNA. Exit.)

(ANNA takes ring to KATIE. Exit.)

(KATIE is sat curled up, back to the audience, rocking. Slowly she turns around. She is holding a small knife,

sobbing, silently. Her arms are covered in blood. Takes ring to **KATHERINE**. *Exit.*)

(**KATHERINE** *puts ring on and admires it. Pours a glass of wine and reclines on the bed reading cruise brochure.*)

(*Effects: gradually fade lights to black-out.*)

End of Play